Joe Camp's
BENJI
at WORK

Ready for action: Benji waits on top of his orange fiberglass kennel.

Joe Camp's
BENJI
at WORK

by Rita Golden Gelman

SCHOLASTIC BOOK SERVICES

NEW YORK · TORONTO · LONDON · AUCKLAND · SYDNEY · TOKYO

For:

Danielle
Michelle
Andrea
Scot
Eric
Rusty
Jamie
Carla
Joan
Lisa
Jan
Mitchell

and the millions of other Benji fans.

Photos courtesy Mulberry Square Productions

ISBN 0-590-31504-8

12 11 10 9 8 7 6 5 4 3 2   0 1 2 3 4 5/8

Contents

On the Set

IT IS 7:15 A.M., barely light out. More than fifty people, most of them in blue jeans and boots, are climbing in and out of trucks, gathering in little groups, talking, walking, running. Cameras are rolling down the street on wheels.

There are crew people climbing on ladders, changing street signs. Others are changing fire hydrants, moving mailboxes, painting props. There are giant, thick, electrical cables all over the place. And piles of wood. And pipes. And sheets of metal.

Down the street, behind one of the giant trucks, is a rented red and white van. And in the van, resting, is the reason for the whole crazy scene: BENJI.

Benji, the lovable mutt that every kid or grown-up kid in the world would like to romp with or snuggle with or run with down a country road; Benji, the famous actor, veteran of movies, TV specials, a documentary, and thousands of public appearances; Benji — the dog with the big, brown eyes — is making another movie.

By ten o'clock, Benji has already filmed his first scene. A man with a gun was chasing Benji down a street and around the corner. Benji ducked into a doorway alcove to hide from the man.

The second scene, which Benji is about to film, picks up from there. Benji is hiding in the doorway. The man stops, looks around. Then the man discovers Benji. He points his gun at the dog. Benji is frightened. He backs away from the man, terrified.

The cameramen are ready to shoot. Benji is standing in the middle of the doorway, waiting, listening.

"OK. ROLL CAMERA. ACTION!"

The man runs onto the scene. He stops, looks around. He sees Benji and points the gun. Benji stares at the man and backs into a corner. There is fear in his eyes. There is fear in the way he holds his body: his tail between his legs, his head down, his muscles tight.

"CUT!"

The cameras are finished. Benji lifts his head, wags his tail. His body relaxes.

"Good Boy, Benji. Good, good, good," says Frank Inn, Benji's owner and trainer. And Benji runs to Frank for his little pea-sized piece of steak and his large, bear-sized hunk of love. Frank feeds him, pets him, pats him, ruffles his fur, and tells Benji over and over what a good dog he is.

Benji is happy. There is a sparkle in his eyes. His little body jumps up and down and wiggles with pride.

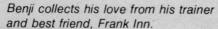

Benji collects his love from his trainer and best friend, Frank Inn.

An extraordinary performance! Benji, the dog, was acting! He wasn't doing tricks, like a circus dog or a show dog. He was playing a part, like an actor. And a good actor too. A good actor convinces you with his whole body that he really is scared or confused or happy. A good actor makes you forget that he is really a person playing a part. He *becomes* the character he's playing.

When you watch a Benji movie, you are certain that Benji is really being threatened by a man with a gun . . . or that he really has fallen in love with a beautiful little girl-dog named Tiffany . . . or that he really is wondering how to solve a problem.

In the scene just described, there is no doubt that Benji, cowering in the doorway, was convincing. You *know* he was scared.

How did Benji know what to do? How do you tell a dog-actor to look scared? Frank Inn, Benji's trainer,

" . . . or that he really is wondering how to solve a problem."

owner, friend, is the man who does the telling.

A person-actor reads his script to find out what kind of a character he is playing. Benji doesn't know how to read. Frank does the reading. A person-actor talks to his director to find out where he should stand, how he should move, what he should do with his body, his eyes. Benji talks only to Frank; Frank talks to the director.

On the morning that the doorway scene was shot, Frank and the director, Joe Camp, had stood in front of the doorway, talking. Joe explained that he wanted Benji to move away from the man, to look scared, to cower. Joe showed Frank where the camera would be set up and where Benji had to stand. Then Frank walked away.

Frank wandered among the bustling crew. He had a glazed, thinking-look in his eyes. How would he do it? How was he going to get the "look-scared" message across to Benji?

Frank considers how he will translate Joe's directions into Benji language.

After a few minutes, Frank walked over to the orange, fiberglass kennel that Benji was resting in. He opened the door and lifted Benji out, petting him, scratching him in the places he knew Benji loved to be scratched, softly talking to the dog.

Benji licked his favorite person as they walked to the doorway, Benji in Frank's arms.

When Frank and Benji arrived at the doorway, Frank put Benji down. It was time to rehearse. No cameras yet.

Imagine the scene: The cameramen are setting up. The lighting people are checking their equipment. There are crew people moving around the small space in front of the doorway.

Frank moves back so that he is out of the camera's way. He takes a blue cloth leash out of his pocket. He narrows his eyes and sets his face in an angry look. Then, in a gruff voice and speaking as fast as he can, Frank begins to shout: "Benji, move back. Back, back, back. Get your head down. Get back, back,

"Back, Benji. Move back!" shouts Frank.

back. Get back. Get that head down. Down. Head down, Benji. Head down."

Benji backs away from Frank and sits down in the corner. "Don't sit down. Get up, up, up. Now get back. Move back. Back, back, back, back."

Frank shakes the leash menacingly. "Get back. Back, back, back."

Benji moves back. His head is down. His body is tense.

"OK, Benji. Good boy. Good, good. You did that good. Good boy, Benji."

Benji jumps to Frank, tail wagging. He eats his steak, collects his love.

They rehearse the scene four more times before Frank is ready to begin shooting. He wants to be certain that Benji knows his part.

Finally, Benji and Frank are ready. The cameras roll. Benji has learned well. With Frank cueing him,

Benji cowers in the doorway.

Benji does it again, this time for the camera. He looks frightened, tense. It is easy to believe that there is a real gun pointed at him and that he really is terrified.

But then, the director yells, "Cut," and Benji runs to Frank and the two of them congratulate each other on a job well done.

Benji gets a well-earned steak bit from Frank.

A Special
Kind of Partnership

FRANK AND BENJI are partners (as well as very close personal friends). Benji needs Frank to explain the scene and to let him know what he's supposed to do. And Frank needs Benji because Benji's the star.

Frank and Benji have a very special kind of partnership. It's based on touching and loving and trusting. It's based on words, on looks, on body movements. And most of all, the Frank–Benji partnership is based on understanding.

Frank truly understands Benji. He knows what makes Benji happy. He knows what makes Benji sad. He knows how Benji will react to a sound or a friend or a stranger or a surprise. It is this special understanding that makes the Frank–Benji partnership so successful.

Take, for example, the chase scenes. All of Benji's movies have scenes where someone is chasing Benji. When Benji was filming his newest movie Frank brought BB along to help out in those scenes.

BB is Benji's niece. She is only two years old. Benji and BB are good friends. But Frank knows a secret about their friendship: Benji can get very jealous of BB. So Frank uses the jealousy to help Benji act out the chase scenes.

The first step in filming a chase scene is to determine where the dog will run. In the scene described earlier, where the man was chasing Benji with a gun, Benji had to run down one block, across a street, and down another block.

Frank and Joe talked about the run. Joe explained to Frank exactly where Benji had to run in order for the camera to film him. Then it was up to Frank and Benji to make it happen. They had two human helpers: Frank's wife, Juanita, and his assistant, Roland. And they had two animal helpers: a dog named BB, and Jackie the Cat.

(left) Frank, with Benji and BB, talks with Joe Camp. (above) Jackie the Cat; and (right) Juanita with BB and Benji. Jackie, BB, and Juanita are three of Frank's helpers.

First, Frank brought both dogs over to see Jackie the Cat, who was in her cage at the place where the chase would end. (BB and Benji both love to play with Jackie the Cat, even when she is in her cage. And Jackie the Cat likes to play with them.)

Frank wiggled the wooden cage. He let the dogs look in. The dogs hopped around, jumping on the cage, sticking their noses into the holes. Cats are fun . . . even in cages. Jackie was having fun too. She knew from experience that BB and Benji would never hurt her.

(right) Benji and Jackie are good friends.
(below) Benji and BB, sniffing and playing around Jackie's cage.

Then the dogs went with Roland to the starting line, BB on a leash, Benji in Roland's arms, Jackie the Cat in their minds. Juanita was at the finish line with the cat. Frank was in the middle, between Roland and Juanita.

A diagram of how the scene is arranged.

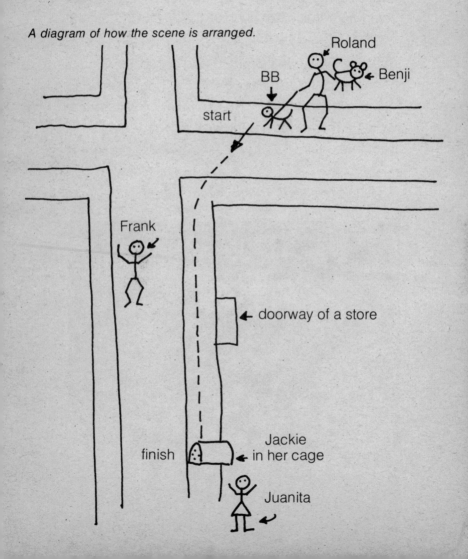

Roland

BB

Benji

start

Frank

← doorway of a store

finish

Jackie ← in her cage

Juanita

When the dogs were in position, Frank began to shout, 'Ssssssssss, ssssssssss, BB, BB, BB. . . . C'mon, BB, c'mon, c'mon, BB, BB, BB, BB, c'mon."

At the first "Ssssss," Roland let BB go and Juanita began to shake the cat cage, loudly enough so BB could hear it as she rounded the corner.

Benji was still with Roland, waiting his turn, but not patiently. Benji knew what BB was doing. She was on her way to play with Jackie the Cat. Benji wanted to play too. It wasn't fair for BB to be playing with the cat while Benji stood still. Benji was jealous and dying to get there, fast.

A test run: BB starts toward Roland as Frank and Juanita hold Benji.

Then came the call from Frank. "Sssssssss, ssssssssss, Benji, Benji, Benji, Benji, Benji . . . C'mon, Benji . . . C'mon, Benji, Benji, Benji, Benji . . ."

Benji takes off after BB.

Benji took off, running as fast as he could. BB wasn't going to play with that cat without him! Benji rounded the corner and practically flew to Juanita, Jackie the Cat, and BB. "Good boy, Benji. Good, BB. Good, good, good." She gave them each a tiny piece of steak. She let them play with the cage. She told them how good they were over and over again.

They rehearsed a few more times. BB always took off first; Benji always got jealous.

Joe and Frank confer while Benji rests.

Then Joe and Frank had another talk. The script called for Benji to run past the doorway of a store in the middle of the block, to stop short, think, "Hmmmm, that looks like a good place to hide," and then turn around and run back into the doorway.

There are two ways to shoot (or take) that scene. They could do it in two takes. Take one: Benji runs past the store; take two: Benji stands still, then turns around and runs into the doorway. Or, they could do it in one take by getting Benji to run, skid to a stop, turn around, and race into the doorway.

Joe wanted to do it the second way. It was more realistic. Why use the best actors if you're not going to take advantage of their talents?

Once again, Frank walked around for a few minutes, thinking. How was he going to get the message across to Benji? How do you tell a dog to skid to a stop, turn around, and run into a doorway? Frank stood still. He walked. He stopped again. Then he smiled. He had it!

Benji and BB went back to the starting position with Roland. They left Juanita and the cat where they had been during the rehearsal.

When the dogs were out of sight, Juanita picked up the cat and quietly walked into the doorway of the store. This time there was no rehearsal. The dogs would run. The man with the gun would run. The cameras would shoot.

Benji and BB go back with Roland.

"ROLL CAMERA. ACTION!"

"Ssssssss, BB, BB, BB, BB, BB. C'mon, BB . . . BB, BB, BB, BB, C'mon."

BB took off. She knew exactly where she was going. She had rehearsed the scene before. She knew that Juanita and the cat would be waiting for her around the corner and down the street.

BB on her way to Juanita and the cat.

But as BB raced past the store, Juanita picked BB up and ran into the doorway. Juanita, BB, and the cat were now in the doorway.

"Ssssssss, Benji. Benji, Benji, Benji. C'mon, Benji. C'mon, Benji. Benji, Benji, Benji." Benji rounded the corner at full speed, pursued by the man with the gun. As soon as he passed the doorway, Juanita called him, "Benji, Benji, Benji, Benji, Benji. C'mon, Benji. C'mon." She rattled the cage. "Benji, Benji, Benji, Benji, Benji . . . . Rattle, rattle, rattle."

Benji stopped short, listening for a second. "Hey what's going on? I thought Juanita and the cat were down the street. What are they doing back there?" Benji skidded to a stop, turned around, and raced into the doorway.

"CUT"

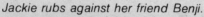
Jackie rubs against her friend Benji.

Frank teaches Benji a new move in their backyard.

Learning to
Follow Stage Directions

A GOOD ACTOR has to know how to take stage directions. He is constantly being moved around on the set. "Turn a little." "Lift your hand." "Swing your arms." "Cross your legs." "Tilt your head."

Benji had to learn how to take stage directions, too. But for Benji, it was even harder than for most actors. Benji had to learn a whole new language!

Frank Inn has been teaching Benji that language since the days when Benji was a tiny puppy. At first, Benji learned the easy words. He learned "stay." He learned "sit." He learned "lie down" and "get up."

Each day, Benji learned more words. And each day Frank tested Benji on the words he already knew. Little by little, Benji added to his vocabulary. "Back up." "Come forward." "Bow down."

Some of the moves that Benji makes on command: "Come forward." "Bow down." "Turn your head." "Rest."

"Sit up."   "Pick up your foot."

As Benji got older, he learned how to take stage directions for more and more complicated actions. "Pick up your foot." "Pick up your tail." "Open and close your mouth." "Yawn." "Stretch." "Speak."

Benji also learned how to work with props. He learned how to open a drawer ("Pull it, Benji. Pull it, pull it, pull it."). He learned how to close a drawer ("Nudge it. Nudge it, Benji."). He learned how to pick something up in his mouth ("Pick it up, pick it up, pick it up."). And he learned how to put it down ("Drop it, Benji. Drop it.").

Like a child learning how to talk, or anyone learning a new language, Benji's vocabulary kept growing and growing and growing. After a while, Frank lost track of Benji's vocabulary. By the time Benji was one year old, he was able to do almost everything Frank asked him to do.

Benji knows how to "beg" with conviction and charm!

Getting Ready for a Career in the Movies

MOVIE-MAKING IS a very strange business. Actors and actresses must be ready to perform in all sorts of situations. Benji, too.

Some facts about movies never change. There are always a lot of people running around on the set. There are sound people and light people. There are camera people, and there are the people in charge. It is impossible to make a movie without a lot of people.

So, Benji had to learn to concentrate with lots of people around. Frank and Benji have a lot of friends. Frank encouraged their friends to come watch Benji work. He never asked them to be quiet or still. He wanted them to walk around, to talk, to act in his backyard the way the movie people might act on the set.

Even today, Benji sometimes works with a yardful of people looking at him. He is rarely tempted to look around at them. He has developed the ability to concentrate on his work — to look only at Frank, unless Frank tells him to look somewhere else.

Benji often works with lights glaring in his eyes.

Benji also had to learn to work with cameras pointing at him and lights glaring in his eyes. He practiced that at home, too. Frank set up a camera in Benji's training area. He set up lights. And Benji learned to get used to those kinds of distractions. All actors must. They are tools of the trade.

Benji lives in southern California where most of the days are sunny and warm. But an actor has to be prepared to make movies anywhere. So Frank had to create different kinds of weather. He set up four sprinklers in his yard, and sometimes Benji worked in the "rain." Frank set up a huge fan in his yard, and sometimes Benji worked in the "wind."

Benji trained at night to get used to darkness. He trained at noon to get used to the sun. He practiced running on a hard driveway and on a gravel road, on grass and on dirt, on dry land and in puddles.

Benji moves on wet, slippery pavement in Greece.

It was also important for Benji to be able to take directions from other people. Sometimes Frank might have to be out of sight and out of hearing distance. So Frank taught the Benji language to Roland and to Juanita. And they sometimes work with Benji too.

Frank has taught the Benji language to Roland and Juanita. (left) Roland with Benji.

Juanita plays with Benji and BB.

Another problem on a movie set is that sometimes Benji cannot see Frank, but can only hear Frank's voice. Frank wanted to be certain that Benji was prepared for that, too. So he worked Benji in a little blue blindfold, made especially for Benji. Benji can follow Frank's stage directions with a blindfold on! Working with a blindfold also sharpens his hearing.

Benji's blindfold. It fits snugly so that it won't interfere with Benji's actions.

Those are some of the very special problems that have to be overcome in order to make any movie. A good actor is well-prepared. But no matter how well-prepared the actor, each new movie brings with it new problems.

*"Pick up
your foot."*

Benji makes some moves on the set while
people watch.

"Come forward. Bow."

Training for a New Movie

IT IS THE end of July. A package has just arrived in Frank's mail. It is the screenplay for Benji's new movie tentatively entitled, *Oh Heavenly Dog*. The movie is scheduled to begin shooting in October.

Oh Heavenly Dog will be the first movie in which Benji does not play Benji. In this movie, Benji will play the part of a man named Browning. Well, not *exactly* the part of a man. The man, Browning, has been turned into a dog. Benji will be playing the dog.

To Benji, a new script usually means that he has to work on new skills. Frank reads the script carefully. He takes notes. In one scene Benji has to take a letter out of a post office box. In another scene Benji has to climb up a fire escape and open a window. In a third scene Benji has to open some drawers and look through them. And in a fourth, he has to take a telephone off the hook and try to dial it.

All of these skills have to be practiced at home. When Benji arrives on the set in October, he must be able to understand Frank's directions and perform them in front of the camera. Frank and Benji have two months. It is time to begin.

The first step is to buy the props. If Benji is going to learn how to open drawers and look through them, Benji has to work with real drawers. If he is going to pick up a telephone receiver, he has to work with a real phone.

Within a couple of days, Frank has set up Benji's props in the training yard. There is an old office desk with a telephone on it. There is a window frame and a post office box. There is a set of drawers with wooden knobs. (Frank knows from experience that the drawers *must* have wooden knobs. Metal knobs hurt Benji's mouth.)

Soon after the props are set up, Frank shows Benji how to grab a wooden drawer knob and pull out the drawer. "Pull it. Pull it. Pull it, Benji. Pull it, Benji.

Benji has worked open a drawer.

Good." And Benji gets a piece of steak and a little loving. "Pull it. Pull it. Pull it. Good Benji. Good boy." And the piece of steak.

At first, they try it with the drawers empty. Then Frank puts a little weight in them. In the movie, the drawers will be filled with papers. Benji has to work gradually toward opening the drawers when they are filled.

Each day Frank and Benji practice. Frank varies the work so that Benji will not become bored. They may spend 10 minutes with the telephone, then 10 with the window, then 15 with the drawers. They work several times a day, doing the same things over and over.

Benji has not had to learn new words for this script. His new actions are actually new versions of old actions. For example, when Benji was a pup, he learned how to "dig it up." "Dig it up. Dig it up. Dig it up," Frank would yell. And Benji would lift up his paw and scratch at the ground.

When Frank studied the movie script to the new film he noted that Benji had several new actions to perform that were similar to "dig it up." In one scene, Benji had to look through some folders inside a file drawer. In another, Benji had to look at a pile of photographs and move them around so that he could see the ones on the bottom. In a third scene, Benji had to try to dial a telephone with his paw. And in a fourth scene, Benji had to try to open a car window by scratching on it.

Benji peers out of a car window after he has "scratched it open."

Benji, listening to his travel agent about a world tour.

Joe Camp's
Benji
in color

A warm reception from fans in Japan.

*Showers of flowers
in Hawaii.*

*The best way to see Switzerland – snuggled
in your best friend's arms!*

Drying off after a good swim.

*Kite flying,
anyone?*

*A movie star enjoys an
afternoon at the beach.*

Watching the passing parade in Paris, France.

(above) Benji in the Netherlands. (below) Driving home from the airport, a dog likes to check the familiar sights.

Even for a pro, traveling can be a headache!

Frank realized that all those movements were the same. They were the "dig it up" movement, where Benji had to lift up his paw over and over again and paw at something. But each new action had to be practiced.

Benji had to be taught that when the telephone is in front of him, and Frank says, "Dig it up," Frank means paw on the telephone. And if Benji is standing in front

"Dig it up" means "paw on phone" here.

of a file drawer and Frank says "Dig it up," he means paw at the files. "Dig it up" in the car means paw at the window. And "dig it up" on top of the desk means paw at the pile of photos.

Benji already knew *how* to "dig it up." Now he had to learn *where* to dig.

Frank also noticed that there were several parts of the script that required Benji to pick things up. Benji had long ago learned how to "pick it up." Now he had to learn that if Frank said, "Pick it up," while Benji was standing in front of a telephone, Frank meant pick up the receiver; and if Frank said "pick up the pencil," he meant pick up the yellow thing around to the left.

Every day, over and over and over again, Frank and Benji rehearsed Benji's part. Over and over and over again.

"Pick it up" means "remove the receiver."

42

A sequence from
Benji's new movie in
which he plays a
detective.

Benji nudges
open the window ...

... looks around
cautiously ...

... the coast is
clear, so he
proceeds with
his investigation.

*Like all dogs, Benji loves to walk with his
best friend. And walking is good exercise!*

The Physical Part
of the Training

MAKING A MOVIE is hard physical work. The day begins at 7 A.M. and sometimes it doesn't end until 7 P.M. The hours, all by themselves, would exhaust most people and dogs. But add to that the exhaustion an actor feels when he has to do the same scene over and over again because something isn't quite right.

Some scenes are taken 10 or 20 times. Some even more. On one "take," perhaps the lights weren't right; on another, maybe there were shadows on the set.

On a third, the dog looked the wrong way. On a fourth, the person had a strange look on her face.

"ROLL CAMERA, Take 1, CUT."
"ROLL CAMERA, Take 2, CUT."
"ROLL CAMERA, Take 3, CUT."
"ROLL CAMERA, Take 10, CUT."
"ROLL CAMERA. ROLL CAMERA."

Every actor goes through it. And every actor had better be in good, strong physical shape.

Benji does a lot of running in all his films.

He has to climb too — things like high stools or fire escapes.

For Benji, that is especially true. In addition to the long hours and the tedium of repeat "takes," there are always strenuous physical demands in whatever part he is playing. The scene that is being shot over and over again may require Benji to run down one street, across another street, and down the block. Or it may require him to climb up a fire escape — over and over and over again.

Frank knows that when Benji starts a new movie, he had better be in great shape! As soon as the new script arrives, Benji goes into training. He runs alongside Frank's motorcycle. He swims in the pool.

He walks on his back legs and does other special exercises to build the muscles in his legs. One of Benji's leg exercises is especially strenuous and very good for Benji's leg muscles. Frank sets up two ladders next to each other. Benji puts his front legs on one ladder and his back legs on another. Then he climbs up both ladders at the same time . . . and back down. By the time the movie goes into production, Benji is ready.

Benji on the alert for the next bit of action.

Shooting a Scene

It is a bright, sunny day in Montreal. Shooting has been underway for nearly a month. Director Joe Camp cannot shoot scenes for his newest film on the street today. It is too nice out! Most of the movie is supposed to take place in London on dreary, misty days. They cannot shoot when the sun is out.

Originally, Joe had wanted to make the film in London. After all, that *is* where the action is supposed to be taking place. But he ran into a problem: in order to bring animals into England, the government requires that they be quarantined for six months. That means that if Benji were to film his

Joe Camp affectionately nuzzles Benji. He agreed with Frank that they couldn't submit Benji to English quarantine regulations.

movie in London, he would first have to be locked up for six months. He wouldn't even be able to live in a house with Frank. He would have to stay in special government facilities.

It seems silly that any government would want to lock up Benji. Certainly he has no diseases that he could give to English animals! But a law is a law and Frank and Joe refused to do that to Benji. So, Joe decided to make the film in Montreal where many of the streets and buildings are very similar to streets and buildings in London.

When the sun is out in Montreal, Joe shoots indoor scenes in the studio. Today's scene takes place inside someone's apartment. According to the script, when the scene opens, Benji is standing on a desk, looking down at a calendar, supposedly to read a phone number that is written there.

After Benji looks at the number, he walks across the desk, over a bunch of magazines and papers, and onto a counter where the telephone is sitting. When he gets to the phone, Benji forgets the number and looks back at the calendar. Then he takes the receiver off the hook, puts it down, and tries to dial with his foot. It is not possible to dial a phone with a dog's foot, so Benji looks around for help. He sees a

Benji puts the receiver down.

Benji tries using a pencil to dial a number.

pencil and picks it up in his mouth, places it in the dial hole, and dials the number. Next, Benji lies down near the earpiece so he can listen to the voice at the other end. He barks into the mouthpiece and hangs up the phone.

Benji listening to a (dull) conversation.

Benji and Frank had practiced this scene at home. Now the cameras were ready to shoot. Here's how they did it:

THE DIRECTIONS: WHAT BENJI IS TOLD	THE ACTION: WHAT BENJI DOES
1. "Benji, Benji," Roland calls. (Roland is off-camera and down low. Benji has to look down to see Roland.)	1. Benji looks down at the calendar.
2. "Go on around there. Go on. That's good. Go on. Go on. Get on over there. Hurry up. Get on over there. Good, Benji. Good. Good." (That's Frank talking.)	2. Benji walks on the desk, across the cabinets and the magazines, onto the counter, and over to the phone.
3. "Benji, Benji." (Roland calls. He is still off-camera and down low.)	3. Benji looks back at the calendar.

4. "Pick it up. Pick
   it up. Pick up the
   phone. Good. Good.
   Pick it up. Pick it
   up. Pick it up.
   Good." (Frank is
   talking again, and
   from now on.)

4. Benji picks up the
   receiver in his mouth.

5. "Drop it. Drop it.
   Drop it down. Drop
   it down. Drop it.
   Good. Drop it."

5. Benji puts the
   receiver on the
   counter.

6. "Dig it up. Dig it.
   Dig it up. Foot.
   Foot. Foot. Dig it.
   Dig it. Dig it. Foot. Foot.
   Foot. Dig it. Dig it up.
   Dig. Dig. Foot. Foot.
   Dig it up. Dig it up.

6. Benji tries to dial
   with his paw.

7. "Get on over there.
   Get the pencil.
   Pick it up. Pick
   it up. Pick up the
   pencil. Pick it up.
   Pick it up."

7. Benji turns around
   and picks up a pencil
   in his mouth.

8. "Get back there.
Head down. Put it
down. Head down.
Head down. C'mon.
C'mon, Benji. Head
down. Get it down.
Get it down. Head
down."

8. Benji turns back to
the phone and puts
the pencil into one
of the dialing holes.

Note: This is where Benji is supposed to dial the phone with the pencil in his mouth. This turned out to be a problem for Benji, for Frank, and for Joe. The pull of the dial was too much pressure for Benji. Joe and Frank tried to rig up a gadget to give Benji help, but the gadget didn't work either. It didn't look real. At the time this book went to press, Joe and Frank still weren't sure how they were going to make it happen. "Benji always comes through," said Joe. "I'm not worried."

9. "Lie down, Benji.
Lie down. Get over
there. Lie down.
Lie down."

9. Benji puts his head
next to the earpiece.

10. "Speak. Speak, Benji. Speak. Speak. Speak."

10. Benji barks.

11. "Put it on there. Get it on. Get it on. Put it on. Get it on. Drop it. Drop it. Easy. Easy. Good. Good. Get it on there. Get it on. Nudge it. Nudge it. Nudge it. Good boy."

11. Benji puts the receiver back on the hook.

The above is one of the most difficult scenes Benji has ever done. He did it in parts, not all at once. It took him three days and dozens of "takes" before he got it just right.

In the movie, the scene will take less than five minutes. Benji will appear totally relaxed as he checks the number, walks to the phone, and uses it. Benji is such an extraordinary actor that no one will ever realize how hard Benji had to work to make it happen.

Filming
Oh Heavenly
Dog! in
Montreal.

A well-earned
rest between
scenes, for
Joe and Benji.

Frank directs Benji in some nimble footwork on the ladder.

Just a Little Bit of Bragging

Robert Redford is a terrific skier. Paul Newman is a skilled race-car driver. Suzanne Somers is a great cook. Many talented actors and actresses have skills in addition to their acting ability. So, it is not surprising that Benji, too, has some very extraordinary skills.

It would not be unusual if you were to wander by Benji's house in Sun Valley, California, and find him climbing up — and down — a ladder.

If it happens to be a hot day when you wander into Benji's backyard, you might find him in the swimming pool. Benji is an expert swimmer and diver. He can climb and then dive off a 14-foot ladder and swim to a shorter rope ladder that is hanging from a double highwire. If you are lucky, you may see Benji climb the rope ladder and walk on the high wires.

Or, if he is asked to, Benji may pull his friend Tiffany on a raft. Tiffany is a fluffy white Maltese terrier who is a movie star in her own right. When Tiffany's ride is over, Benji will pull the raft to the side of the pool so Tiffany can climb off.

If Benji is not working, and you don't see him around, he is probably inside the house, asleep on the couch.

Benji is resting, but he keeps one eye open. He doesn't miss a thing!

The Things
an Actor Has to Do!

Making movies is only a small part of Benji's job. Like most famous actors, Benji spends a lot of time traveling, making personal appearances, and attending benefits.

Take, for example, Benji's involvement in TOYS FOR TOTS. Every year the United States Marine Corps sponsors the collection and distribution of toys to poor children all over the country. In 1978, they asked Benji if he would be co-chairman, with Gavin McLeod, of the nationwide campaign. Benji accepted.

*The space uniform is confining, but Benji
is happy to share honors with Gavin McLeod
in the signing ceremony. His Toy for Tots
is on the next page.*

The Marine Corps set up a press conference to announce Benji's participation. Because the Marine Corps is a part of the astronaut program, they decided that Benji should appear at the press conference in a space costume.

A designer was hired to make Benji's costume, and Frank and Benji arrived at his studio for the fittings. With Benji in his arms, Frank stepped into the fitting room. It was filled with bolts of material, racks of yarn, and people-forms for fitting people-costumes. There were no dog-forms.

Benji stood on a table and the designer took out his measuring tape. He measured Benji's body from nose to tail. He measured Benji's height, his legs, his shoulders, his tail, his head. Benji didn't enjoy it very much, but it was all part of a day's work and Benji stood still.

The major problem of the day was whether to put Benji's tail in or out of the costume. They decided to let it hang out and the designer designed a tail-hole in Benji's space costume.

On the day of the press conference, Benji — in his space costume — presented the first toy of the campaign to a Marine astronaut. What was the toy? A stuffed Benji, of course.

The stuffed Benji is soft and huggable, like the real Benji.

Benji has done more traveling in his four years than most people do in their whole lives. He's been to Japan, Italy, Switzerland, Canada, France, Venezuela, Greece, Germany, Netherlands, and Puerto Rico. And he's visited most of the states — including Hawaii.

Benji among the flowers of Hawaii.

Benji poses in front of a windmill in the Netherlands.

Benji feels at home, wandering through the streets of Athens, Greece...

Benji always knows when he's about to go on a trip. He watches Juanita getting everything ready. He watches, impatiently, while Frank loads up the van.

*. . . in fact, Benji is at home in any cosmo-
politan European city, whether it's in
Greece or Italy or France.*

Benji doesn't take very much with him when he
travels. He might take a raincoat and some boots and
a bunch of squeak toys. He doesn't need much. He

doesn't need piles of makeup and curlers like many stars. Benji's is a natural beauty. His fluffy white eyebrows are supposed to flop over his big brown eyes. The scraggly black hair on his ears is supposed to be scraggly.

Frank lovingly grooms his shaggy friend.

Sometimes Frank dabs a little after-shave lotion on Benji's fur before they go out. It makes Benji smell good. Benji hates it. He runs into the bedroom, climbs on the bed, and tries to wipe it off on the pillows.

At first, Benji really did want to wipe off the smell of the lotion. But after a while, the whole thing turned into a game. Whenever Frank took out the lotion, even before the top was off, Benji raced to the bed and wiggled around on the pillows.

Benji, snug in his traveling case.

Benji may not like the after-shave lotion, but he loves to travel. Sometimes he rides through airports on the top of a baggage cart. But he never goes into the baggage compartment. Benji travels in his own, open-sided suitcase. And he always flies in the first-class section of the plane.

Often, the pilots and the crew come to say hello. They pet him. They fuss over him. And Benji loves it.

He loves it when they travel in different countries

and people recognize him on the street. Frank knows that Benji loves affection and Frank nearly always lets people pet Benji. And when Benji fans ask for Benji's autograph, Frank hands them a picture of Benji signed with a paw print.

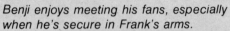

Benji enjoys meeting his fans, especially when he's secure in Frank's arms.

Benji enjoys eating (and drinking) with Frank.

Benji goes to the fanciest places, all over the world. Often he is invited to banquets where he sits at the head table. His manners are nearly perfect.

Benji sits at the table with a napkin around his neck and he eats with the people. There is only one flaw in his behavior. After dinner is over, and Frank is making a speech, Benji curls up on his chair and goes to sleep. He's heard it all before.

Why?

What is it about Benji that makes people love him? Why do they crowd around him, go to his movies, reach out to touch him? Why do they call to him in French, in Japanese, in German, in English? "Is that the real Benji?" they shout. "Can I touch him?"

Wherever Benji goes, people give him gifts and awards. He has fireplugs and fancy collars, plaques and sheriff's badges. One town even gave him a tiny tree. Benji has a bone made of pizza and a gilded bone, and a hat and coat that were made by a 13-year-old girl in Hawaii.

Love for Benji crosses all lines. Kids love him. Adults love him. Fancy people love him. Shaggy people love him. People all over the world know and love Benji. What is his secret?

Children as well as adults all love Benji. He is a lovable, huggable mutt whom everyone loves to pet.

Part of it is that Benji is a star. His movies have made him famous. Part of it is that Benji is a legend. His movies have earned more than 66 million dollars. But stardom and wealth cannot create love.

Benji's special magic, his real appeal, is that under all the glamour, he's a mutt. His shaggy eyebrows flop over his eyes. His fur sticks up in all directions. He could be anybody's dog. He's just a lovable, huggable mutt. His face always looks as though it's smiling. His eyes, those wonderful big brown eyes, have love in them. It is impossible to look into Benji's eyes and not want to snuggle him.

Benji the dog, Benji the star, is just a lovable mutt who likes to make people happy. And no matter where he goes, that's exactly what he does.

Benji Statistics

FULL NAME: Benji

BIRTHDATE: September 3, 1975 (Benji's father
played in the original movie.)

BREED: Undetermined, but probably fox terrier,
cocker spaniel, poodle, schnauzer, lhasa
apso, and maybe more

PROFESSION: Actor

WEIGHT: 21 pounds

MEASUREMENTS: HEIGHT — 15 inches
NOSE TO TIP OF TAIL —
34½ inches
TAIL — 11 inches
EARS — 6 inches

EYES: Brown

FAVORITE FOODS: Steak, chicken, fish

FAVORITE TOYS: Rawhide chewsticks and
squeak toys (especially when
they're someone else's)

FAVORITE GAMES: Tugging with his puppies on
old, knotted-up socks
Playing ball

BEST FRIEND: Frank Inn

LIKES: Sleeping on Frank's pillow
Riding in the car
Visiting people

DISLIKES: Getting fitted for costumes
Smelling like after-shave lotion
Babies, when they pull his hair

HATES: Fighting
Meeting strange animals

LOVES: Affection

Joe and Benji share a tender moment.

Like other celebrities, Benji rides in an open car, acknowledging his fans. Here, he drives with Frank in Frank's red Porsche.

Take a bow for a great performance, Benji!